BOROBUDUR

BOROBUDUR

The Buddhist legend in stone

BEDŘICH FORMAN

MAGNA BOOKS

Acknowledgments

For the generous support I have received I would like to express my gratitude to the Department of Information of the Republic of Indonesia in Jakarta, the Archaeological Institute in Jogjakarta and to all those who offered me advice and encouragement. In particular to Z. Dubovská, M. Krása, V. Miltner, and V. J. Žižka.

I should like to give particular thanks to Mr. Anthony Gardner, London, as well as to Spink & Son Ltd, London, who kindly gave permission to photograph several of their artefacts for this book.

Photography and text by Bedřich Forman

Contribution "Borobudur – A message in stone"
written by V. J. Žižka
English translation by Till Gottheinerová
Graphic design by Bedřich Forman

This edition published 1992 by Magna Books,
Magna Road, Wigston, Leicester, LE18 4ZH,
by arrangement with The Promotional
Reprint Company Limited.

ISBN 1 85422 387 9

Printed in Czechoslovakia
2/11/04/51-02

Contents

For my brother Werner Forman, with whom I visited and worked on many monuments of ancient cultures in four continents. Without his many-sided contribution and aid, this book would not have come into being.

Author's note

In the last hundred years, a large number of remarkable books have been published on the subject of Borobudur, one of the outstanding Buddhist monuments of the world. They have shed light on many of its different aspects — historical, architectural, artistic, religious and philosophical.

When, aware of this fact, I decided to present Borobudur in yet another book, there were several reasons for my doing so. In the first place, the majority of the publications mentioned were intended, in scope and conception, for specialists and did not reach the broader circle of readers. The geographical position of Borobudur may well have played a part in this. While Angkor in Cambodia and other sanctuaries in Thailand, Burma and elsewhere in Asia are known to lay persons interested in reading about such things, Borobudur meant something only to experts and to a very limited number of laymen. This is due to its being on an island and to its relative inaccessibility.

But the main impulse for this publication was simple enough. Borobudur is not only a mysterious monument to Buddhist education, it is not simply a picture of the cosmos according to Mahayan Buddhism, nor is it just an immense picture book illustrating the life of Buddha. In a word, Borobudur is beautiful.

And if I speak generally about messages handed on through architecture, then this applies equally to Borobudur, for its message was written in a particularly calligraphic way; it is my firm belief that one of its numerous messages is that of beauty itself — beauty in the broadest sense of the word.

It is the modest aim of this book to present readers with a close-up picture of Borobudur and to help them discover its beauty, generally acknowledged but, unfortunately, rarely demonstrated in pictures.

Bedřich Forman

Time and space

From the moment when man abandoned his cave shelter and began to fashion a dwelling for himself with his own hands, he attempted to invest this functional activity with a metaphysical meaning. It is characteristic that, at first, this attempt was more often linked with the resting places of the dead than with the homes of the living.

Palaeo-archaeology and palaeo-ethnography have provided new evidence that, even in the earliest phase of his spiritual development, man was aware of phenomena that existed independently of his will, to which he tried to adapt or submit. Our ancestors of long ago must undoubtedly have had certain ideas on matters such as time and space, on the future, and on their likely place in it. Such were the ideas which gave rise to religious ceremonies and, with these, a philosophy which permeated art and architecture. Tombs, sanctuaries and buildings serving astronomical purposes and secular structures provide convincing enough proof.

It is, therefore, no exaggeration to say that the great majority of important buildings of all ages were intended to pass on to future generations something of the philosophy of each epoch. These messages are varied in content and broad in scale. They range from knowledge empirically acquired in the search for the ideal structure, given by climatic, morphological and functional conditions, to data derived from geometry and arithmetic with their symbols. They include much religious symbolism. They span time and space in a mighty arch, right down to our own age, represented by the Atomium at the World Exhibition in Brussels in 1958 — witness to the fact that man had penetrated the secret of the basic structure of matter.

It is difficult to decide what it may be that our era will be able to pass on to future generations, and whether we might not in fact be responsible for all information about ourselves being wiped off the face of the earth. But it is an irresistible and fascinating duty to try to decipher the bequests of the past and to pass them on to those who will pick up the baton after us.

The path of this relay race is lined with countless milestones upon which is inscribed, in indelible writing, a great deal of what we are now doing our utmost to comprehend. One of these milestones in time and space is Borobudur, a structure that preceded the Atomium by twelve whole centuries and which holds the key to another great concept of the human spirit.

Question marks of time

We know of buildings and whole urban areas which, on being uncovered, seem voluntarily to give us an insight into their past. Even if archaeologists and historians have often to expend great efforts to confirm the picture gained, existing sources provide much corroborative evidence on which to draw. The situation is different in the case of objects that stubbornly guard their incognito and, when they do permit the veil over their identity to be drawn aside, they reveal only their external face, so posing many further questions.

Among the former we might include many tombs in Egypt, Mesopotamia, Herculaneum and Pompeii which have provided us with sufficient facts in writing and works of art. The second group includes the still enigmatic buildings of the Mayas in Mexico and in the virgin forests of Yucatan and the as yet unexplained and mysterious city of Zimbabwe in Africa. Among them ranks also the great Buddhist sanctuary outside the Indian sub-continent, Borobudur on the island of Java—a structure that holds a unique place in the history of world culture.

Like those buildings of America and Africa, Borobudur was thoroughly investigated during its reconstruction at the turn of this century—perhaps more thoroughly than most, thanks to the great efforts of a number of leading scholars. We should here recall the names of N.J. Krom and T. van Erp and of their disciple A.J. Bernet Kempers, W.F. Sutterheim, J.G. de Casparis and Claire Holt, among others. At the present time, the largest ever work of restoration and investigation is afoot, instigated a few years ago by the government of Indonesia under the auspices of UNESCO with contributions from many countries. The first stage of renovation is to be finished in 1981. In spite of thorough, long-term investigations, Borobudur has retained many of its secrets and still poses fundamental questions today. No clear-cut answers have yet been given to many of its enigmas despite a number of clever hypotheses, beginning with the significance of the name Borobudur, the precise dating of its origin, its meaning and its function.

The limited scope and purpose of this book prevents closer examination of these questions. But it will be useful to give a brief outline of the historical background of Buddhism on Java and the genesis of Borobudur, despite the relatively good condition in which it was discovered, continues to pose so many questions to specialists of many professions.

We shall leave aside the prehistoric period before the arrival of the Aryans, who brought their culture to the original inhabitants, the Dravidas, and turn to the oldest written sources. These are in the form of liturgical texts, originally handed on by word of mouth and later recorded in writing under the general term of 'Veda', meaning divine knowledge. They are immense in scope and are clearly the work of many generations. Experts have traced the first of the Veda to the second millenium BC, but opinions vary greatly. They may have come into being even earlier.

The Veda, as a set of theological texts, reflects the thoughts of the priests — the Brahmans. For this reason it provides little information on secular life. The Veda is divided into two sets of unequal size: the Veda proper — the older book known as Rig-Veda — and the later one which includes the writings of the Brahmans and the Upanishads. In them appears a host of deities and supernatural beings. A considerable part of the texts is devoted to rituals and how to conduct them. Other parts contain philosophical theses with a description of the universe: according to this, the world has two parts, one placed above the other — the Earth and the Sky — or even three parts — the Earth, the Sky and the Air. Elsewhere this number is trebled and there are three Earths, three Airs and three Skies, making a total of nine — later to become one of the sacred numbers of Buddhism. Experts have deciphered in the Rig-Veda that the Aryans thought the Earth and the Sky were linked by some kind of axis. The Earth is described as a square — the four sides joining the four cardinal points. These and many other aspects are of interest to us in connection with the unsolved questions surrounding the symbolism and meaning of Borobudur.

As time passed, the religious and philosophical views of the Aryans, as taught by the priestly caste of the Brahmans, began to be influenced by the views of the earlier inhabitants — the Dravidas. Brahmanism then gave rise to the genesis of Hinduism — in the words of H. von Glasenapp — 'that multifarious and in its totality unique religious and social system which, to this day, links the majority of Indians'.

In the first half of the first millennium BC, two systems took shape among the many other religious and philosophical schools that were not strong enough to find their place by the side of Brahmanism. Together with Hinduism, these two systems form the three main religions of India. One is Jainism — historically represented by Mahavira, who lived several decades before the coming of Buddha — with which Buddhism has much in common. The youngest of the three is Buddhism, which has spread far beyond its original homeland.

These three main religious systems gradually underwent a complex process of amalgamation so that they share many common elements. The basic ethical goals of all three came to be much the same, and the main difference between them lies in the means by which these goals are reached. The common aim of all these teachings is to liberate man from the endless succession of birth, death and rebirth, to surmount *karma* and to attain a state of bliss.

The Jainists do not acknowledge the authority of the Veda and other writings of the Brahmans and have a canon of their own, which has been preserved to this day without any major changes. The Buddhists, on the other hand, adopted certain elements of Brahmanism. Their teaching underwent a great many changes over the centuries, which gave rise to more than one type of Buddhist teaching.

The trinity of these great religions determined the shape of the social and cultural life of India over a period of 2,000 years, and no substantial changes occurred in this time, even under the impact of Islamic culture at the beginning of our millenium, which elsewhere left such a striking mark upon the local culture. The teaching of the three religions spread far into the heart of Asia, and Hinduism and Buddhism were major influences in south-east Asia and the Far East, reaching as far as Sumatra and Java, China and Japan.

The Stupa

In India more than in other parts of the world the religious and philosophical doctrines determined the order of life, of thinking and of art over thousands of years. Architecture and sculpture held special places of their own, as visible proof of what was originally handed on by word of mouth and later in writing.

The rules of architecture inscribed in the sacred books of the Śilpaśatra, dissertations on sculpture and painting perpetuating the instructions of the deities in the sacred writings of the Tibetan Tanjur, and a number of other works together laid down the basic principles of Indian architecture.

One of the oldest forms of Indian architecture — which has a direct relation to the subject of this book — is the 'Stupa', known in Ceylon and other countries of Hinayana-Buddhism by the name of 'Dagoba', in Burma as 'Pagoda', and in the realm of northern Buddhism, in Tibet and the Himalayan region as 'Chorten'. Originally the Stupa was a tumulus — a mound of piled-up stones or soil — which, in the Neolithic and Bronze ages, marked a burial place and contained the relics of Buddha or a Buddhist saint. Later it became a reliquary, and later still a symbol of Buddhist cosmology.

Although the Buddha was strictly opposed to any kind of worship of his own person, Stupas were built in all places of religious importance in the first centuries following his death. As Buddhist teaching spread afar, their popularity reached the most remote places. Stupas can be found under the equatorial sun of Java, and swept by the icy winds of Tibet and Mongolia. They may be as large as the biggest cathedrals, or so small as to be held in the palm of the hand in the form of tiny votive offerings.

Contacts and impulses

It is not yet entirely clear when and how the first contacts between Indian culture and the original culture of the Indonesian archipelago took place. It is held — by G. Coedès among others — that a major role was played by the trade contacts that grew between the countries of south-east Asia. The first trade pioneers may first have travelled along the coast of eastern India, then across the Malayan peninsula and finally as far as Sumatra, Java, and Borneo, bringing the local inhabitants their more developed culture and, with it, the precepts of the Hindu and Buddhist religions.

This, of course, remains a matter of hypothesis. According to F.W. Wagner, it is possible that, under the growing pressure of the Guptas, who ruled over a large part of northern India roughly between the third and sixth centuries AD, some Indian princes may have moved their courts to the remote islands beyond the reach of the reigning dynasty. The Brahmans or Buddhist priests would have gone with them.

One might also argue that Indonesians occasionally visited India. They would then have brought back the influences of Indian life and religion to their own country, or might even have invited Hindu or Buddhist scholars to their homes.

Whatever the case, the discovery of Sanskrit inscriptions from about 400 AD in Borneo and Western Java proves that the influence of Indian culture on the islands was already significant at that time. The first contacts must have occurred much sooner, however, as is shown by the discovery of three Buddhist statues with characteristic marks of Indian Amaravati sculpture in the second century AD. They were found on three Indonesian islands — Sumatra, eastern Java and the Celebes.

Gradually, the local culture, which was already fairly well developed, became enriched by Indian culture. Before long this was reflected in daily life: new agricultural practices were introduced; the elephant and possibly also the water buffalo made their appearance as draught animals; the horse was imported; the potter's wheel was introduced and changes occurred in the technology of certain other crafts.

Some scholars attribute the introduction of all these novelties solely to the Indian influence. But, given the active trade contacts made possible by robust seafaring vessels, these influences may also be ascribed to other civilizations — notably those of China, the Kingdom of Champa (in today's Vietnam), Polynesia, and others.

According to a generally accepted theory, the Indonesian archipelago was settled some time in the third to second millennium BC by people from Yūnan in southern China. This migration, which in the view of the prehistorian R. von Heine-Gelder lasted about 1,500 years, passed through eastern India, a region with a number of advanced cultural centres, such as Dongson. These connections are strikingly exemplified by the Moon of Bali or, as it is called after the site on which it was found, the Pèdyèng Moon, the largest kettle-drum in the world. The bronze cylinder is one and a half metres in diameter, and about two metres long. Its walls are only a few millimetres thick and the outside is adorned with a magnificent relief of astral ornaments. The Moon of Bali is a beautiful example of the highly developed art of metal casting. This type of work is typical of that produced in Dongson towards the middle of the first millenium BC.

It remains a matter of hypothesis as to whether this masterpiece, unique both in its technology and as a work of art, was imported to Bali or made there. I believe, after examining the drum in situ and fragments of a cast that was found close by, and after having seen the Dongson finds, that the drum was made on Bali itself. Together with other outstanding artefacts, it shows that the Indonesian archipelago was, for a long time, the meeting place of many great cultures and that the people there always managed to add their own influence, thanks to their own powers of invention.

Hinduism and Buddhism did not escape the Indonesian influence and, as time passed, they developed specific Indonesian traits. Both these ancient religions were adopted in Indonesia and, in turn, the Indonesian creative vitality was imprinted upon them, especially in the field of the arts. The word 'confrontation' is often used to describe the meeting between the cultures of India and of Indonesia. It would be more fitting, however, to speak of a confluence, not of two but of many different cultural influences.

This is the only way in which one can explain the origin of many works of architecture and sculpture of the Hindu-Javan epoch. And it was thus that Buddhism, after five hundred years of influencing and assimilating other cultures, acquired the prerequisites to build Borobudur, in which the teachings of Buddhism, deep in the heart of the Indian civilization, and the Indonesian genius loci created one of the great peaks of world art — a symbol of life, humanity and beauty, a symbol of time and space, a symbol of the universe.

Borobudur

Barely 150 years have passed since amazed European eyes first gazed upon Borobudur. We do not know what caused it to have been abandoned for almost two centuries after its completion. This may have been due to changes in the dynasties and related changes in religion, the cult of Siva having become dominant. An explanation may lie in the as yet obscure function of this piece of architecture. There is even a theory that recalls the fate of some of the buildings in Mexico at the time when the Spaniards first arrived, suggesting that when, in the fifteenth century, Islam conquered the mighty Kingdom of Majapahit, Borobudur was deliberately hidden under a layer of soil to be spared from the iconoclasm of religious fanatics. There is, however, quite a good chance that the tropical climate, together with tectonic and volcanic activity, saw to it that this jewel of architecture became covered under a layer of soil and thick vegetation.

10   The seasons, years and centuries passed over Borobudur in its abandonment.

But this sacred place lived on in the minds of the people. Generation after generation spoke of its marvels and the one-time memories turned into a legend that wove its web around the mysterious hillock. At the beginning of the last century this legend apparently reached the ears of Europeans and so, in 1835, the protective layer of soil and overgrowth was removed from Borobudur, and one of the most magnificent cultural monuments was reborn.

One of the puzzles surrounding this monument is the question as to when it actually came into being. The original dating — between the years 750 and 850 AD — based on the style of certain architectural details, has now been given greater precision. On the basis of the Praśasti — inscriptions carved in the stone — which have now been discovered, de Casparis places the completion of construction work in the reign of King Samaratunga of the Shailendra dynasty which lasted from 775 to 864 AD.

The Shailendra dynasty ruled over a large part of Sumatra and its influence spread as far as the eastern parts of India. Its rulers practised the Buddhism of the Mahayana school, a type of Buddhism that was widespread in northern India. Its texts were written in Sanskrit, in contrast to the Hinayana school whose texts were written in Pali. This dynasty was probably responsible for the construction of the majority of important Buddhist monuments in central Java.

Another inscription deciphered by de Casparis suggests that in 842 AD the daughter of King Samaratunga devoted certain lands and rice paddies to the maintenance of Borobudur. On the basis of these two inscriptions, and taking into account the dynastic genealogy, de Casparis deduced that the year in which Borobudur was consecrated was, in all likelihood, 824 AD.

Authors are greatly at variance in the interpretation of the very name of Borobudur. Some, such as T. Bodrogi, translate it as 'countless Buddhas'; de Casparis attributes it to the second part of the name Bhumisambharabudara, which means 'mount of the accumulation of the virtues of the Bodhisattva'. Dr Claire Holt is of the opinion that it might contain a dual interpretation: 'mount with a series of terraces' and 'King of mountains' or 'mount of the King of mountains'. The Shailendra dynasty originates from the dynasty of the 'King of mountains', which reigned in the Kingdom of Fu-nan in continental south-east Asia in the first half of the seventh century.

Indonesian sources suggest that the name Borobudur might be a composite of two words: the word 'Budur' as a place name, and the Sanskrit word 'vihara', meaning monastery, which later became 'byhara' and then 'bara'. If this were the case, the name Borobudur would simply mean 'monastery at Bodur'. This name appears in the mediaeval Javan panegyric *Nagarakertagama.*

There is one more simple explanation: an Indonesian equivalent for the word 'hillock' or 'mount' is 'budur' and, together with the word 'bara', Borobudur could simply mean 'monastery on the hill'.

A great deal of interest has been shown in the function and meaning of Borobudur in many publications. All these papers have one feature in common — namely that everything concerning Borobudur is mere hypothesis.

Borobudur is usually considered to have been a monument in glorification of Buddhism, a place of meditation for both priests and laymen. If this enormous stone building was the central part of a monastery, it is possible, even likely, that the rest of the monastery was made of wood and fell victim to the ravages of time and the climate. Remains of wooden buildings, which have been found on the north-west side of the grounds, support this theory. Borobudur might, therefore, have been a place where Buddhist priests were trained and, as was often the case in India, it may also have been a centre of pilgrimage.

It may simply have been erected as a symbol to proclaim the faith of the fervently religious. Or it may have been built by the ruling monarch so that he might identify himself with a Bodhisattva — a man of enlightenment who declined to become a Buddha so that, in his subsequent lives, he might show the people the path to true wisdom. This would seem to be confirmed by the iconographic stress on the Bodhisattva in the spirit of Mahayana Buddhism. Another theory is put forward by de Casparis in the first volume of his work *Praśasti*: he suggests that Borobudur might have been either a 'Chandi', a mausoleum for the ashes of eminent secular persons and saints or a mere monument.

11

Whatever purpose Borobudur really did serve, recent interpretations of its symbolical significance concur in one respect: that this monument is a unique symbol of the universe according to Buddhist cosmology.

Harmony

When describing the architecture of Borobudur, other factors must be taken into account — for example, its location in the surrounding landscape. Borobudur forms an integral part of the panorama and is, at the same time, its dominant point — a feature that is typical of Asian architecture. In the broad valley surrounded by long mountain ridges and several active volcanoes, there reigns a very special peace, a sense of salvation and liberation from all earthly ties.

It is certain that the builders of Borobudur did not leave the choice of site to mere chance. It was selected with a special feel for beauty and an understanding of counterpoint. There is a striking contrast between the untamed forces of the volcanoes and the rich, peaceful life pulsing in the broad valley aptly known as the 'Paradise of Java'. And high above it all, there is the sky, untouched by either of the two counterpoints — the sky towards which, since time immemorial, the longings of mankind have risen and to which man comes closer as he ascends Borobudur.

Hindu and Buddhist architecture show a preference for sites close to rivers. The confluence of two rivers was considered to be sacred, as, for example, the confluence of the Ganges and the Jamuna in India. Borobudur was built on the confluence of two rivers — the Progo and the Elo, running south into the Indian Ocean.

Today Borobudur is a monument that stands on a hillock in the centre of a lowland covered in palm groves and rice paddies. But was this always the case? Recent Indonesian geographical and geological research shows that this lowland used to be flooded by the River Progo. Borobudur is often compared to a flowering lotus, the symbol of Buddhist teaching. From here it is but one step to the assumption that the builders might have selected this spot intentionally to make use of the two rivers to create a lake around the hillock. The resulting appearance would then correspond to the Buddhist image of the world: the earth rests upon the surface of the world's ocean — 'the Lotus of the Jewel on the Lake'; in its centre there rises Mount Měru around which the sun, the moon and the stars orbit. The sea surrounding the earth is itself banked by a wall of mountains (chakravala).

If we compare this hypothetical picture with the real landscape, we find that the two correspond: there is a little hillock (the earth) with the central Stupa of Borobudur (Mount Měru) in the centre of a depression (the sea), surrounded on all sides by mountains (see appendix No. V).

In a building of such universal conception, astronomical considerations must have played a far from insignificant role. It is quite possible that certain straight lines that link the corners of the multiple twisting galleries with points on the Menoreh mountains may be more than mere coincidence. There is also a probable correlation between the central Stupa and astronomical aspects at certain dates in the year.

Before we give a description of Borobudur itself, let us turn to two minor sanctuaries which are assumed to have been associated with the main temple. These are Chandi Pawon and Chandi Mendut, lying roughly on the east-west axis of Borobudur a few kilometres away. Both these sanctuaries date from roughly the same period as Borobudur. Chandi Pawon lies in the little village of Brayanalan, slightly south of the confluence of the rivers Progo and Elo, while Chandi Mendut lies southeast of this confluence near a tiny village that bears the same name. In contrast to Borobudur, the inner areas of the two sancturies can be entered from outside. The smaller of the two, Chandi Pawon, was consecrated to the god of wealth and affluence, Kuvera, and perhaps built in memory of King Indra, the tenth ruler of the Shailendra dynasty. Today the interior of the sanctuary is bare, none of the original sculptural ornaments having survived. Inside Chandi Mendut, there are three monumental statues of the Buddha and two Bodhisattvas, which must rank among the most beautiful works of Javan sculpture.

According to J.G. de Casparis, Mendut means something like 'temple in the centre of a bamboo grove', while Pawon in the Javan language means 'kitchen' — a place with a hearth where sacrifices may have been burnt before undertaking the ascent of Borobudur.

Although Chandi Pawon is one of the smallest sanctuaries in central Java, architecturally it is among the most beautiful. The concluding photographs in this book are witness to the dignified beauty of Chandi Mendut and its imposing statues and give an idea of the special atmosphere that reigns inside the sanctuary.

Temple — pyramid — Stupa

Borobudur is not a temple in our sense of the word. There is no interior area that can be entered. In Buddhist terminology it is an enormous Stupa. It is, in fact, a pyramid built around a natural hillock.

Above the square double base, 153 metres (502 feet) in length, rise four galleries, decreasing in size by steps. Their walls are adorned with a strip of 1,460 large figural and 1,212 smaller decorative panels in bas-relief, of a total length of over five and a half kilometres. There are innumerable other features — gargoyles, portals and little chapels, in which 504 figures of the Buddha and Bodhisattvas are seated.

Above these galleries there is an area of almost 2,000 square metres (about 21,500 sq. ft) with a series of concentric terraces. These have no relief decorations. They form the basis for 72 Stupas with a statue of a seated Buddha in each of them, slightly bigger than life size. The first and broadest of the circular terraces is encircled by 32, the second by 24 and the third by 16 Stupas.

The crown of the entire structure is the last terrace with a mighty, centrally placed Stupa, almost 11 metres in diameter. This Stupa has an interior space where an unfinished statue of the Buddha is to be found. It was not necessarily built at the same time as the rest of the building. This interior area, like the smaller one above it, cannot be entered from outside.

The entire structure is laid out to coincide with the four cardinal points. The galleries and terraces can be reached by four stairways leading straight up the centre of each side of the building. Although the stairways and their portals — a total of 25 — barely differ one from the other in size and ornamentation, the eastern entrance is considered to be the main one. For it is here that the climb up this entire mountain of hard andesite blocks begins. According to data published by van Erp, there are more than 56,000 cubic metres — over 2,000,000 cubic feet — of such blocks.

It is assumed that a whole army of workers was needed for so exacting a task. By way of comparison, Dr. Claire Holt gives the estimate of the leading French scholar G. Groslier, who calculated the time and human labour needed to build the Khmer sanctuary at Bantay Chmar in Cambodia, which is smaller than Borobudur. She writes that, with a view to the technical construction facilities of the time, the building work at Bantay Chmar must have lasted 21 years, assuming the work of at least 30,000 stonemasons, 15,000 persons responsible for transport, 4,000 builders and 1,500 sculptors.

Pilgrimage and goal

According to the Buddhist canon, the visitor must ascend from gallery to gallery and make the round of each of them in the direction of the sun's movement. This means that the inner wall of all the galleries remains on his right side. On it, as on a stage, there unfold scenes from the life of Buddha, on an endless strip of relief work — his birth (or rather his last incarnation), his search for wisdom, his enlightenment, his death and the ultimate attainment of Nirvana, the highest state of bliss.

In the course of this pilgrimage along the four galleries, the spectator's view is restricted on both sides by walls covered in relief work so that his concentration is not distracted by anything else. When, after the last gallery, absorbed in the illustrations of this gigantic picture book, he comes out on the platform, he is offered an overwhelming view of the great landscape, with its indescribable, constantly changing colour scheme. And, as he ascends higher and higher up the terraces as far as the main Stupa, his view constantly broadens and he is overcome by a feeling of relaxation, calm and peace. The sky is close and earthly toil somewhere far, far below.

It is not easy to describe the effect of this emotive experience in words — it might be easier to do so in music. Some years ago I spent the long winter months in a Lamaist monastery and later with a Buddhist hermit in the mountains above the Gulf of Tonkin and had the opportunity to listen to two kinds of sacral Buddhist music — eerie cosmic compositions for woodwind and percussion instruments, and ethereally gentle music in monochords. Both might possibly convey the miraculous atmosphere surrounding Borobudur.

For a full understanding of the uniqueness and the meaning of Borobudur, it is necessary for one to know the hieratic and narrative elements of Buddhist art. Only in this way can one decipher the message of the reliefs and the symbolism of the entire structure. Even if the ultimate key to it will remain beyond us for ever, let us try to approach it as closely as possible. Certain moments in the life of Buddha, which constitute the main content of the reliefs, will help us to understand the plot of this unique stone book.

For us the history of Buddhism begins with Gautama Buddha, who is generally considered to be the founder of Buddhism but who was in fact, according to Buddhist hagiography, its last prophet. He was preceded by many 'enlightened' Bodhisattvas who, in similar manner, were seeking and pointing the way towards Nirvana.

The life of Buddha

Gautama was the son of Śuddhodana, of the aristocratic Śakyas, and his wife Maya. They lived between 550 and 450 B.C. at Kapilavastu in northern India, not far from the border with Nepal. His father was called 'King', although he may only have been the leading personality in the local government administered by the aristocracy.

Gautama was not born in Kapilavastu, but in a little village, Lumbini, in its vicinity. His mother had gone to see her parents before the confinement and gave birth on the way. The event is said to have been preceded by several supernatural happenings. The birth of the future Saviour was announced to his mother in a dream in which a white elephant visited her. The birth itself was accompanied by a special glow in the sky, and the gods were dancing, rejoicing and blessing the child. The great saint, Asita, foretold his future greatness.

The boy was given the name of Siddhartha, which means 'the completion of purposes'. Gautama is the name of a Vedic sage and prophet which the Śakyas had adopted as a sign of respect. Siddhartha is sometimes called 'Sakyasinha' — 'the lion of the Śakyas' — or 'Sakyamuni' — the 'sage of the Śakyas'.

Maya died seven days after the birth of her son, and Siddhartha was brought up by her sister Mahaprajapati, Śuddhodana's second wife. He grew up amid great wealth and was duly married to his cousin Jashodhara. His father saw to his education and indulged him in luxury and court entertainment, for he hoped that his son would become ruler and not a saint who would renounce the world, as had been prophesied.

But all the measures his father took to prevent him from getting to know misery and poverty proved to be in vain. Siddhartha stole out of the palace on secret outings and the gods appeared before him in the form of an old man, a sick person, rotting corpses and finally an ascetic. The prince, who had never set eyes on the like, inquired of his companion what the meaning of these happenings was and, on receiving an explanation, returned to the palace, deep in thought. After the fourth outing he received the news that a son, Rahula, had been born to him. Then he is said to have called out: 'Rahula is born unto me; bonds have been clasped upon me.' His decision to seek the way of salvation was not changed by this event.

In the middle of the night, after bidding a silent farewell to his sleeping wife and son, he secretly left the palace on his horse Kanthaka. His sole companion was his faithful groom Chandaka. When he reached Anuvaineya, he got off his horse, laid aside his jewels and exchanged his valuable garment for a simple one made of bast and offered by a deity disguised as a hunter. He then sent Chandaka back to Kapilavastu to convey his decision to his disconsolate father and his weeping wife.

He was 29 years old when he abandoned home and family and went forth to seek wisdom for himself. First he went to the Brahman ascetic, Arada Kalama, and became his disciple. But his teaching gave him little satisfaction, so he sought out another teacher by the name of Udraka. When he did not find what he was seeking even there, he undertook a pilgrimage through Maghada. On reaching Uruvela, on the banks of the River Nairanjana, he settled down and gave himself up to strict asceticism, hoping to gain wisdom in this way. He lived an increasingly abstemious life and, in the end, he consumed only one grain of rice a day, but the enlightenment he had been longing for did not come to him. When he almost died, he recognized that self-torture on its own was not the answer. The five ascetics who had hitherto followed him with great admiration turned away from him, convinced that he had gone astray. Once again he was abandoned and utterly alone.

One night, as he was sitting under a fig tree, he suddenly saw what it was that he had been seeking for seven years. He looked around him and saw that the ways he had trodden in previous lives had led him off the right track. He had a vision of the 'four Sublime Truths' on pain, its origin, how to check it, and the way that leads to overcoming it. In this manner the Gautama turned from a Boddhisattva — 'a being longing for conversion' — to the Buddha — 'the Awakened One', 'the Enlightened One'.

For some time he continued to live in the place where he had reached the longed-for goal, and then he decided that he must go forth and tell the people of his teaching. In vain did Mara — 'the Evil One' — appear before him and tempt him to pass to Nirvana without revealing the 'Sublime Truths' to the people.

The first people whom Buddha converted were two merchants who offered him food. But he weighed up who was to be his first disciple. His former teachers were no longer alive. Then he remembered the five ascetics who had witnessed his .endeavours to find the greatest truth. With his inner eye he knew that they were at Benares, so he set forth and found them in the Rishipatana garden, not far from the town on the Ganges. At first they did not acknowledge him, but all of a sudden they felt the strength of his personality and the change that he had undergone. They came out to meet him and showed him their respect for him. At that very moment, Gautama appeared before them as the highest Buddha, who had passed beyond the wheel of sorrowful lives. He preached his famous Benares Sermon, which contains the quintessence of Buddha's teaching. So it was that the five ascetics became his first disciples. Soon they were joined by others and, before long, the Buddha community consisted of 60 adherents and continued to grow steadily.

Until his death, the Buddha moved tirelessly from place to place throughout his homeland Magadha (Bihare) and converted many people. The most eminent among his lay followers was Bimbisara, the King of Magadha, who performed many good deeds for Buddha and his disciples. Other followers that are often mentioned include Śariputra, Mandgalyayana and Ananda, who is sometimes compared to John the Baptist. A Judas was not missing from Buddha's circle either: this was his own nephew Devadatta, who tried to assassinate him because he refused to appoint him as his successor. When this attempt failed, Devadatta tried to stir up trouble. According to the legend, he finally begged the Buddha for forgiveness. Gautama also persuaded his own father to follow his new teaching, and he became honoured as a saint. He welcomed his son into his community and his stepmother Mahaprajati withdrew from the world and became a nun.

The Buddha spent over 40 years travelling from place to place throughout north-eastern India. When he was 80 years old, he fell ill in the village of Beluva near Vesali. But he recovered and continued along his way to Pava, where he found shelter in a mango grove belonging to Chunda, the blacksmith. According to the legend, Buddha was taken ill again after consuming a meal of pork or mushrooms. Painfully, he made his way as far as Kushinagara where, after making his last will and testament, he passed away.

Borobudur
Pawon
Mendut

1 The same enchanting picture since time immemorial: sunset on the coast of southern India. It was from here that, about 20 centuries ago, the first Indian colonists set off. They took leave of the shores of their homeland and, led by the constellations, they set sail in a south-easterly direction to the remote islands of Indonesia. It was the beginning of a new chapter in the cultural history of India and Indonesia.

2 On the islands, rich with beauty and natural wealth, the alien seafarers met kind and hospitable people who soon accepted their presence. Their culture and religion soon became part of Indonesian culture. The fusion of the two cultures led, over the course of several centuries, to its most beautiful manifestations in the form of Buddhist and Hindu architecture.

3 The Kedu landscape in the central part of the island is often called the 'Paradise of Java'. It was here, below the Menoreh mountains and surrounded by palm groves and rice paddies, in an area with a very special contemplative mood, that Borobudur was built, probably in the ninth century — a Buddhist monument that is unique in the world.

4/5 Buddhism brought many interesting customs from its original homeland — among them that of placing small clay votive tablets in the foundations of sacred buildings. These in themselves are often masterly pieces of relief work. They depict the Buddha, Bodhisattvas, other eminent personalities, sacred places, Stupas or hermitages. They include prayers and quotations from holy writings.

The upper of the three plaques depicted was found on Java; but it may have been imported, perhaps from Burma. It depicts

Buddha sitting in a small sanctuary similar to those found on the reliefs of Borobudur, surrounded by ten small and two larger Stupes. The outline of this plaque was inspired by the leaves of the Bodhi tree under which Buddha gained enlightenment. The lower two plaques come from Indonesia and date from roughly the same time as when Borobudur was constructed. The lefthand one probably depicts a Bodhisattva, the right-hand one the Buddha sitting on a flowering lotus blossom. A nimbus can still be detected around his head, and in the background a sacred text. The two circular plaques form the lower part of a double votive offering in the shape of a Stupa. (See appendix No. IV.)

7 The first impression that Borobudur makes upon anyone who approaches it for the first time is a confusing jumble of horizontal lines, pyramids and cavities, and contrasts of apparently incoherent geometrical shapes. Light and shadow intensify this impression and the eye seeks in vain for a point on which to rest. The stairway in the centre of each of the four sides alone points the way towards an understanding of this heterogenous unit.

6 This view from the height of the clouds shows how ideally Borobudur fits into the surrounding landscape and gives a good idea of its architectonic layout. The basic platform spreads around a natural hillock and above it four galleries rise and recede in terraces with another smaller platform above them, on which can be seen the three concentric circular terraces with 72 smaller Stupas: in their centre stands the main Stupa, today ending in the mere torso of a pyramid, once the base for a mighty stone sunshade, the symbol of dignity and glory.

◀ ◀

8   Corners and lines in thousands of dimensions, always linked at right angles and always according to the cardinal points — this, together with the symmetry of the axes and the concentric arrangement, forms one of the basic principles of this construction.

9   The square ground plan is divided into 20 projecting (positive) and 16 inner (negative) corners: in other words, it forms a pattern in the form of a rough square with 26 corners in all. The floors of all the galleries are arranged in an identical manner. The resulting shape resembles a many-sided crystal.

10/11 As one approaches, the edges of this immense crystal come alive and, on the ground floor frieze that encircles it like a ribbon almost half a kilometre (about 500 yards) in length, there appear symbolic figures, enormous gargoyles in the shape of the heads of sea-monsters upheld by small creatures. From the depth of small sanctuaries more than 500 Buddhas and Bodhisattvas look out, and the overall silhouette is shaped by hundreds of small Stupas.

12—14 One of the decorative infills of the frieze: in the centre stands the demon Raksasa with two female figures. On both sides, there are girls with flowers. Here we encounter for the first time one of the sculptural peculiarities of Borobudur — the deep reliefs of the figures, combined with the elaboration of the draperies of ribbons and veils in the background.

The mighty heads of the sea-monster Makara — with horns, elephant trunk and tusks — form the ends of the balustrades of the stairways and guard the entrances from all four sides from evil spirits.

A solemn, serious mood engulfs the pilgrim who is about to ascend such a stairway. On returning home he will never in his life forget this experience.

12 13 | 14

15

16

17

18

15 The upper relief depicts the Son of God (top left) descending from the sky to announce to the four Buddhas the arrival of Gautama Buddha. The event is set in the gazelle grove of Rishipatana at Benares. The three Buddhas sit on lotus thrones below the crowns of trees. The fourth Buddha (right) is floating on a lotus — about to depart to Nirvana.

The lower panel depicts two scenes which form the frame for the Buddha legend. On the right, on a covered bench, sit a pair of Nagas, apparently the parents of Prince Janmasitraka. The son is sitting at his father's feet and is telling him how he was saved. The left half of the relief shows how Halaka, the hunter who saved the prince, is being feasted. Halaka is sitting in the Pendapa — a covered verandah — as guest of honour and is taking food that is offered to him. On the left, behind him, a man is sitting with a blue lotus blossom in his hand.

16 Manohara's escape from the palace — another of the myths surrounding the life of Buddha. The main front of the palace is on the left, suggested by a stairway. The nymph Manohara is floating in the air — depicted by a cloud — followed by birds. On the left, there is a group of courtiers and guards.

17—20 The descent of the Bodhisattva to earth (top relief). 'When through all his merits he gained the "Lion Throne", he sat upon it and surrounded by a hundred dozen million gods, Nagas and Yakshas he set out upon the journey. One hundred and ten dozen gods bore him with their own hands in a double pavilion and supported him with their own shoulders and hips and a hundred dozen Apsars (heavenly fairies) played for him on human and divine instruments and extolled his deeds.' This is the way this important event is described in the Buddhist legend. The whole scene takes place in heaven, depicted by a layer of clouds above the pavilion; the figures are not kneeling, as it might seem, but floating. On both sides of the pavilion, payongs — broad fans in the shape of leaves, lamps and flowers which serve as sun-shades — are held aloft.

Prince Sudhana, one of the many mystical figures of the Buddhist legend, is bringing his father the tribute of the rebels (lower relief). Sudhana is sitting in front of his father with a tray on which precious objects are heaped. The father is lying on a couch with a canopy, in the relaxed position of a person resting. He is about to grasp the objects offered to him. Behind the couch, there are two female and two male servants. Sudhana is followed by three servants with further gifts and in the foreground, below the trees, there are courtiers, soldiers and bearers of the royal insignia: a large fan of bird feathers, fly-whisks and a parasol. In the right-hand corner, there is another fan made of a large leaf.

21   When the winter season came to an end, the Bodhisattva descended from heaven to earth where, in the form of a white elephant, he entered the womb of his mother Maya. According to Maya's dream, 'he was brilliant as snow and silver, had six tusks, a lovely red head and a beautiful trunk, a springy step and legs as strong as a diamond. He was a magnificent elephant.'

This sculpture depicts part of the palace and Maya surrounded by servant-girls. Either Maya is dreaming or the scene depicts her just before her confinement. In the lower half of the relief, armed guards stand on both sides of the entrance.

23 Maya's palace and guards. The stairway is like that of Borobudur with a decorated balustrade in the shape of a chimera. Above the entrance we can see the head of the demon Kala. Both these creatures are to prevent evil spirits from entering. The palace is crowned with an emblem of a lance with three blades, depicting the might and strength of the spirit. ▶

24 King Śuddhodana, Buddha's father, is going to see his Queen in the Asoka grove (detail). Maya is in her palace with her servants. In the bottom right-hand corner, there is a guard with a sword and, above him, a chamber-maid fanning her mistress. Two servant-girls are coming out of the lower storey, one of them bearing a vase. Three court ladies are kneeling in front of the Queen and handing her jewels on a dish. ▶

22 Manohara is relating one of her adventures to her father, King Druma. The details of the relief depict the King's retinue. The figure on the right holds a parasol, which is badly damaged. Another can be seen behind the elephant. The differences in physiognomy are remarkable.

21 | 22

25—28   Prince Sudhana is undergoing a test among 1,000 Kinnari — mythical beings, half bird and half woman — he is to find his loved one, Princess Manohara.

25   The Kinnari are here depicted as women, sitting in a Pendapa or covered verandah. Sudhana stands deep in thought before them and is about to make a decision.

26   One of the Kinnari.

27   Prince Sudhana.

23   24   25 | 26   27   28 ▶

28   King Druma, who is to give his daughter Manohara to Sudhana in marriage, is watching Sudhana undertake the test. On the left, there is a standard with a winged shell, bird feathers and ribbons.

30—32 Sudhana and Manohara are sitting on a broad couch with a canopy and are watching dancers. On the left there are musicians, at the bottom men with flutes, drums and cymbals and behind them women with smaller cymbals. On the right, you can see the bearers of the parasol and fans and behind them a pair of horses and an elephant decorated with a headband and bells. ▶

29 The Kinnari are drawing water for a bath for Princess Manohara. The spring below the tree is full of lotus blossom. On the right-hand side, one of the Kinnari is kneeling in front of Prince Sudhana, who is about to drop his ring into a dish — a sign for the nymph Manohara.

33—34 Two details depicting how the Brahmans were rewarded for interpreting the dream. The detail ▶
on the left depicts a dignified Brahman on a seat below a palm tree accepting gifts. One of his assistants is
holding the robes he has received and other remuneration — perhaps money — in a little bundle. Another
is holding a parasol. The picture on the right shows the palace of the person who made the gift, King
Śuddhodana — the father of Gautama Buddha.

The beauty of this relief — as that of the preceding one — is particularly striking in its detail. The skilful
mastery of perspective and the elegance of the flowing outlines indicate that both reliefs were made by
one and the same artist.

35 Manohara and Sudhana — not included in the detail — are handing gifts to the people at Panshala. Their entourage is seated at the bottom, together with the bearers of the obligatory insignia — armour-bearers with swords and shields and a saddled elephant.

36/37 These two photographs are details of the relief on which the royal pair are shown with a picture of a man. The upper one shows the left corner of the panel with part of the armed companions of the donor and an elephant with a Mahout — an elephant driver — holding an Ankus — a pole with a spiked point used to control the elephant. The lower one depicts the noble donor with the picture. The man in the picture, perhaps the donor himself, holds an 'Utpala' — a blue lotus — in his raised left hand.

38/39 These two details are taken from the relief that is
the companion to the preceding one. The King seems to be
accepting a picture of a charming young lady or princess.
But it is not clear whether the picture is a gift for the King
or from the King for someone else. The latter would seem
to be suggested by the departing ship on which the sails
have been hoisted. Both the donor or receiver — or poss-

ibly the messenger of noble birth who is to deliver the picture — and the girl in the picture have their hands raised in greeting (Sembah). It is clear that the depicted person enjoys a rare respect, from the fact that a sunshade is raised above the picture of the girl. This sunshade is a mark of status.

40 This is the central part of a relief depicting a noble pair — perhaps a local regent and his wife — talking to two visitors (not shown here). The relief has been greatly smoothed down and is covered in moss and encrusted with lime and salt. But even in this state, its beauty and charm are outstanding. What is clearly visible is the sash that used to be a favourite way of supporting the spine or lower limbs. The King's bracelets have survived in good condition. On the left, behind the King, is a stand with a vessel on it from which smoke or flames from burning incense are rising.

41 This relief shows a nobleman with a rosary sitting in a room in front of an altar. Smoke or flames from burning incense are rising from a vessel in the shape of a lotus blossom. The pavilion is possibly part of a larger complex of buildings. This seems to be indicated by the fence in the lower part of the relief. To the left, below the tall tree, one can make out an entrance and part of another building and, above the pavilion, two parrots.

42 The miracles at the palace of King Śuddhodana at Kapilavastu. 'During the nine months before the birth of Buddha thirty-two miracles occurred. Young lions descended from the slopes of the Himalyas and entered the city of Kapilavastu and without delay took their places by the palace gates. Five hundred young white elephants came and touched the King's legs with their trunks. The children of the gods were sent to play in the palace of King Śuddhodana. And twenty-nine other wonders occurred.'

Here we can see two of them: the divine children playing with King Śuddhodana and the little elephants, with one of them touching the King's legs.

43 The right half of this relief shows a man in a simple garment but with a halo — in all likelihood a Bodhisattva; he is sitting in a mountain landscape indicated by cube-shaped forms on the left-hand side. On the right, there is a lion and an elephant which is about to touch the saint's arm with his trunk. Another animal is coming out of a cave above a little river with fishes in it. There are trees in the background with birds flying above them.

44—46 Queen Maya can be seen on the upper panel going with her companions to the park at Lumbini. The legend relates that there were eighty-four dozen carriages and hundreds of brightly dressed people. In the sculptor's condensed form, the scene is more modest but nonetheless suggests the colourful spectacle to the observer who is familiar with the legend.

The lower relief depicts a noble woman making sacrifices in a small temple. On both sides of the building, there are either decorative ribbons or the smoke of incense burning on the altar. On the left, beside the pavilion, a woman with a large flower in her hand is kneeling. In the right half of the relief we can see the companions of the woman who is making the sacrifice. Two women in the background are bringing further offerings. Palms and other trees give a decorative effect.

45 46

47 This detail shows with what skill and love the unknown craftsmen approached even the least important parts of the reliefs. The armed entourage of a noble person has been worked with the same care as the main part of the relief. Even the smallest details have been joyfully created — jewels on the head of a person who is turning his back, the ear of an elephant and its highly decorated tail, knots with which a fat Mahout sitting on the elephant has bound his garment, and so on.

48 King Śuddhodana is holding his son on his lap after the death of Queen Maya. After the more formal subject matter of the other reliefs this one is touching in its intimacy.

49 This detail, too, has an atmosphere of calm privacy. The noble pair and their servants are sitting in a small pavilion. Six tails form the roof decorations of the pavilion. The exceptionally strong capitals of the columns holding the thin roof of the pavilion are interesting for their combination of different elements: heads of the sea-monster Makara, whose enormous muzzle (mostly they have trunks) protrudes from the head of a lion, and a flower hanging from the muzzle, which is part of the plant motif formed by the lion's tail.

50 The charitable King Uposhada is sitting in a Pendapa with his wives. Behind it, the carved back of a throne is visible. On the left, a servant is bearing away a trunk full of gifts. The person sitting in the foreground is a counsellor or the chancellor of the King's treasury.

51 The King is personally presenting gifts. On his left stand his servants, holding vessels with gifts, and on his right a group of people who are receiving the gifts.

52 The Queen participates in distributing gifts. She is sitting on a throne with a beautifully carved back in a richly adorned tripartite pavilion. We can see two trunks to the right.

53 The Śakyas are demanding that the prince be sent to a monastery for his education. The little Gautama is sitting on his father's lap in a Pendapa where Śuddhodana is receiving members of the family to hear their requests.

51

52

53

54 King Śuddhodana with a flower in his hand, is leaving for a hermitage. The servants are carrying him on a sedan-chair. The procession naturally includes a Payong bearer — here indicated only by an arm holding the sunshade. Dignitaries on horseback precede the bearers with drawn swords, then there is a standard bearer and, in the background, an elephant on which a Mahout with a mighty Ankus is sitting. The procession is led by armed guards. A person has emerged from the hermitage and is greeting the royal procession respectfully with his hands raised (Sembah).

55/56 This is one of the 16 curves of the first gallery. On the top, in a small niche, there is a statue of Buddha slightly larger than life size and, above the corner, a projecting gargoyle with the head of a monster. On the upper relief, the King and Prince Gautama make their way to the temple. On the lower relief, the King is sitting in a mountain region and holy water is being offered to him. (The content of this relief differs considerably from the liturgical texts — a different explanation might therefore be possible.)

57 The birth of Prince Mandhatar. King Uposhada with the Queen and the small prince are receiving a man in a royal robe — perhaps come to congratulate them. He is sitting on a low stool in front of the King. His retinue stands behind him.

58   The prophesy of the birth. The royal couple, the prince and their servants are listening to the words of a Brahman, who is sitting on a low stool below a large fan of bird's feathers.

59 Teaching at school. Pupils with volumes of lontar — books made of palm leaves —
are sitting in a small Pendapa and are quietly listening to the teacher's words. The silence
is indicated by the doves on the roof.

60—62 Śakra's visit. On the opposite side a figure in the robes of
a king or god is kneeling in front of the young King Mandhatar. The
man with a cap with an elephant trunk and ears holding an Ankus on
his shoulder is Airavata, Śakra's counsellor. From this it can be deduced that the visitor is no less than Śakra himself. Behind King
Mandhatar (top), sits the Queen and, between them, perhaps another of the King's wives.

63　A bearded Brahman requests the prince in an eloquent gesture to make a sacrifice. But his posture suggests hesitation. His counsellors (bottom right) and his wife sitting next to him are probably supporting the Brahman's request. Below the tall seat is a square dish containing food.

64　The Bodhisattva is giving Gopa a ring: 'and then all young girls of the great city of Kapilavastu gathered in the audience room where the Bodhisattva abided. This one then gave all girls beautiful jewels and decorations. The girls who had received their gifts could not bear the glitter and lustre that surrounded the Bodhisattva and set off home. Then came the girl Gopa of the Śakya clan accompanied by her slaves. But the Bodhisattva had already handed out all his jewels so that there was none left for Gopa. With a smile Gopa turned to him: „What evil have I done, oh prince, that Thou dost not want to make me a gift?" And the Bodhisattva replied: "No evil hast Thou done, but Thou art the last to come." Then he took a ring off his finger, the last of a hundred thousand gems, and gave it to Gopa.'

We can see the Bodhisattva in a tripartite pavilion as he is handing the ring to Gopa. The vases and the peacocks on the roof and the opulence of the roof itself and its supporting pillars show the wealth that surrounded the prince.

65/66 The Rain of Garments: one of the great miracles in which
— as in the Rain of Corn and the Golden Rain — garments are
falling from the clouds. The prince is sitting on a cushion in a small
Pendapa and watching how his subjects are trying to gather as
many garments as possible. The clouds, out of which the clothes are
falling, form a highly decorative relief. The two men sitting in front
of the prince on the left belong to the court and are therefore not
taking part in the lively scene.

67/68 Prince Mandhatar goes out to conquer the world. At the head of the expedition are seven jewel-bearers. The two royal jewels, the discus and the gem, lie on a lotus blossom, which can be seen above the elephant head (top left). The King (right) holds a flower in his right hand. None of the figures is touching the ground with his feet, which indicates that the expedition moved in the air. On the other page is a detail of the two shield-bearers.

69—71 Another corner of the gallery shows us, on the top relief (which is difficult to distinguish), Gopa sitting in the centre, defending herself for going out without a veil. The King is sitting on the right and between him and Gopa are two men, who look like Brahmans, perhaps her accusers. Behind Gopa on the left is one of her servants.

The lower relief may depict the burial of Mandhatar's remains, though this is still a matter of uncertainty. In a fenced-off area stands a pavilion, perhaps a small sanctuary. On the right, below the trees, are a woman and a man — noble persons judging by their clothing. The woman is expressing respect in the 'Sembah' gesture, either to the man with a tall tiara, or to an object in front of her. This object has sometimes been indentified as the Jewel — the symbol of happiness — and it is also possible that it is the urn containing Mandhatar's ashes. But it seems most likely that it is a gift — perhaps a fruit on a dish — which is being offered in sacrifice in front of a receptacle containing the earthly remains of the King.

73 A sea-going ship with cross-rod and tiller. The crew is working on the main yard and helmsman is sitting by the helm. Above the ship is the sky, on the left a decorative cloud.

72 Musicians in the ladies' chamber in the Bodhisattva's palace. At the top, women are playing stringed instruments known as the vina and the cithara and, at the bottom, the drum, flute and a hand-drum.

74/75 These are two of the three palaces of the Bodhisattva. King Śuddhodana has decided to build for his son, the Bodhisattva Siddhartha, three palaces: a cool one for summer, a warm one for winter and, for the season of rains, a palace that will provide both cool and warmth. Depicted here is a room in the palace for the period of rains with Prince Gautama (Siddhartha) and two women. On the next page is the summer palace, with a woman who is looking into a mirror and doing her hair.

76/77 Top right: the first of Siddhartha's outings — his encounter with an old man. The groom informs Siddhartha that all living beings must succumb to age.

Bottom: two phases of the same story are here depicted in one unit. On the right, a falcon is sitting in a tree, hoping to still his hunger, and a dove sits on the back of the Bodhisattva's throne. The Bodhisattva turns down the falcon's request with a gesture of his hand. When the falcon objects that he is doomed to die of hunger, the Bodhisattva solves the problem by promising him flesh from his own body. On the left, we see that the Bodhisattva did not break his promise: on one side of the scales sits the dove and, on the other, the Bodhisattva is making his sacrifice — part of his own body. Tension can be seen in the faces of the participants. On the right, by the scales, is a payong and, above it, an arrow-holder. It is interesting that such scales, with a weight and columns, can still be found today in the more remote areas of Java.

78 The upper panel depicts Siddhartha's second outing — his encounter with a sick person. On this badly damaged relief the emaciated figure of the sick person can be quite clearly made out in the left-hand corner.
The lower relief depicts the worship of a god or Bodhisattva.

79 A girl on a sedan-chair made of fabric and two bamboo poles. The bearers are village folk and a Raksasa — a guard with a club — is huddled below the sedan-chair.

80 Swan and Fowler.

81 A slave girl is rubbing the resting ruler with scented oil. There are four birds on the roof.

83   Two sequences from the fable of the 'Lion and the Woodpecker'. On the left, the lion is begging the woodpecker to remove a bone from his throat, and on the right the woodpecker is trying to do so.

84   An audience with the King or Prince.

◀ 82   Top: Bodhisattva in his bath. A hundred thousand sons of the gods fill the river with scents and flowers drop from the sky. In the top left, Brahmans are dressed as ascetics. This event is clearly taking place in a mountainous region.
Bottom: Hiru lands at Kiruka. Again there are two phases of the same event in one picture. On the right we see a big ship on a voyage on the open seas and, on the left, the emigrants after landing. In the background there is a house belonging to local inhabitants.

85 An audience with the Bodhisattva, who is sitting on a chair called 'Sinhasana' or 'Lion Throne' and marked with a symbolic lion among the draperies. On the left, there are courtiers and two bearded Brahmans. In the background there are two large fans — one made of bird's feathers, the other of leaves — and a sunshade.

86 Scene from Buddha's last banquet. The Buddha is sitting on a chair with his right hand raised in the 'Mudra Vitarka' gesture and surrounded by his followers. Among the men a figure with a smoking incense-burner is sitting closest to Buddha; behind him stands a man with a dish and a brush. On Buddha's right, there is a little table with incense. Both the women and the men are holding food, flowers and gifts in their hands. This relief ends the pilgrimage around the first gallery.

87   A noble lady at her toilet. The scene probably takes place in the evening because bed servants with torches are standing between the pillars. Under a wide bed there are two chests, reminiscent of a small casket (see pict. 137).

88   Megha, an Indian guru, is sitting below a big tree and talking to Sudhana, who is sitting in front of him on a low stool with a flower in his hand. Apsars (heavenly fairies) are floating above them and dropping flowers and a wreath upon them.

89   Sudhana and Ratnachuda. Ratnachuda is sitting in a beautiful pavilion. Servants stand on either side and below them there is a little lion on the pedestal of the pavilion. In the centre, in small niches, are three little elephants. Sudhana is sitting in the centre next to a vase of flowers; his hands are folded in the 'Sembah' gesture. His companions are in the right-hand corner of the relief. In the background two ornamental trees resemble brooches or buckles; a bell hangs in the left one and both are crowned with small sunshades. A big Payong with a tail is standing in the centre. Above the trees are parrots and one flying Kinnari. The upper edge of the relief is adorned with a strip of garlands and parrots.

90 Sudhana and Nala. Nala is sitting in a luxurious building on a small throne. Beside him on the floor is Sudhana. Each one has a servant by his side. The pavilion is decorated with tails and long feathers. Next to the pavilion is a palm tree with fruits and below it a guard with a drawn sword.

91 Sudhana and Smantanetra are sitting in a little pavilion adorned at the top with a mask of the demon Kala and on both sides with representations of the sea-monster Makara who has a bell hanging from his open mouth. Similar masks are situated above the stairways of Borobudur.

92 Detail showing two noblemen and their retinue.

91 92

90

93 Worshipping the Stupa. Two noble persons are making offerings on the altar below the Stupa. The front of the altar facing the spectator might be the real top panel of an altar with a vessel of offerings in the centre and incense-burners on the sides, with smoke rising from them. A heavenly nymph is dropping flowers from a cloud. The Stupa rests on a lotus blossom and an architrave upheld by two lions. The Stupa itself is decorated with a strip of garlands and, on its pinnacle, there is a sunshade. The central Stupa of Borobudur is adorned in exactly the same manner.

94 Here, too, we can see respect shown to a Stupa. This time it does not stand in the open as on the preceding relief but inside a small temple; it has 13 sunshades above it. The plinth of the small temple is adorned with a strip of tortoises moving towards the left as a symbol of the slow but steady movement around the Stupa. In the small Pendapa adorned with peacocks, the person making the sacrifice is sitting with his companions.

95/96 These two details depict a specific Javanese concept of figural relief work and are typical samples of the handiwork of the builders of Borobudur.

97 The pilgrim is now on the third gallery. The relief above the Bodhisattva, sitting in a small niche, depicts the Bodhisattva in conversation with a follower, who is himself a saint, judging by the nimbus.

98 Visit in the 'Little Temple of Bells'. Above the complicated construction of the sanctuary, two Kinnari are floating. The visitor is a king or Bodhisattva. This beautiful relief is not in good condition; it is flatter than most of the rest and very damaged.

99 Conversation below garlands of lotus.

100 A small section of the relief 'Visit to the Second Lotus Temple'. The work is badly damaged, but the detail reveals its former beauty.

101/102 Maitreya's charity. The Bodhisattva Maitreya descended from heaven to give presents to a group of simple Brahmans. He is standing on the left and, behind him, two servants are holding a dish with money and a box with rings. The noble spectator on the right is holding a lotus blossom. The side volutes are still remarkably rich in detail with flowers and birds, despite the fact that they are badly damaged.

103/105   These three views are taken from places where butterflies occasionally come to rest. They show the rows of small and beautiful reliefs, mighty heads of gargoyles, antefixes at all projecting parts, statues of Bodhisattvas in the niches and finally the forest of Stupas of all sizes that rises above it all. Time, the sun and rain have covered the surface of the reliefs with a patina of moss and lichen.

108 Homage to the Bodhisattva Samantabhadra.

◀ 106 The 'Jewel' — in the fourth gallery — symbolizes happiness. In the highly geometrical presentation, one can see some form of rocky cavern in which five strange shapes are to be found. The largest of these rests on a lotus blossom in the centre.

◀ 107 The scene of 'Worshipping Buddha and the Bodhisattva'.

109   111 | 112 ▶
110

109 The pilgrimage among the pictures of the life of Buddha draws to an end.

110 The last relief of the Bodhisattvas looking down upon the pilgrim who has only to pass through the last gate . . .

111/112 . . . from the last gate he can see his goal . . .

113 Here suddenly the chaos of shapes and impressions disappears. A view far into the distance opens up before amazed eyes. Somewhere, deep down below, is earthly life with its toil, its many questions and its few answers, its fears and its uncertainties. An inner voice requests that a short stop be made — one begins to get a sense of order. The top platform, which might fittingly be called 'a stop on the path to knowledge', grants rest after the exacting climb up the galleries. It is here that the last part of the pilgrimage begins — the visit of the three terraces on which stand 72 Stupas and, above them, the last and biggest Stupa — the symbol of the Buddhist centre of the universe.

114   The perforated bells of the Stupas on the first terrace . . .

115/117 . . . finally bring the Buddha within reach of the pilgrim. It is no longer the Buddha of the stone pictures on the lower storeys, full of joy and secular bustle — here the pilgrim stands face to face with Buddha the Enlightened One.

The simple circular terraces, adorned only with Stupas, symbolize the difference between 'the soul' and 'the senses' and contrast with the highly decorated galleries of the lower storeys. In this conception one can see the main content of the whole monument as well as its individuality in the Buddhist architecture.

118   A thousand-year-old dialogue of forces.
The statue on the first terrace without its cover.

119 The daily orbit of the sun changes Buddha's smile.

120 Traces of time and the atmosphere. *The surface of a stupa on the second terrace.*

121—123 A partially dismantled Stupa shows the position of the statue of the Buddha and the structure of individual sections of stone. Stupas on all three terraces cover these beautiful statues of the Buddha sitting in a lotus posture with different gestures of the hands (Mudra) — suggestive of certain spiritual symbols.

126 The local people assert that Borobudur changes colour like the light on a dew-drop on the lotus. The midday equatorial sun does not cast long shadows, but adds a further tone to the palette of colour changes.

127 Blocks of the central Stupa. Like the whole enormous building they are loosely placed one upon the other and there are traces of putty in the fissures dating from the period of reconstruction of Borobudur.

128 Here the beauty of these special constructions is seen at its best — the shining light literally encompasses their elegant outlines and, together with the background of distant mountains, forms a picture of harmonious calm, characteristic of all great monuments of Asia.

◀ 124/125 The calm on Buddha's face.

129/130 The blue Menoreh mountains from the foot of the mighty central Stupa of Borobudur. Whoever reached this height, after a meditative pilgrimage called 'Pradakshina', was rewarded.

This is the view from the third terrace over the kedu valley in the westerly direction. 'Pradakshina' means 'Ritual deed' and, during it, the object of worship — a sanctuary or person — is encircled in such a manner that it remains on one's right-hand side.

131/132 An afternoon shower fills the valley with the scents of the tropical island and conjures up a small rainbow above the Stupas of Borobudur. The quiet and peace of a sacred place reign all around.

133/134 The shadows are growing longer. For the last time the flames of the 'Tree of Fire' shine below the groves of coconut palms and the entire region becomes veiled in the twilight atmosphere. Above the valley rises the lonely thousand-year-old symbol of Buddhist erudition — the majestic main Stupa of Borobudur.

135 What the age-old sacred texts proclaim, nightfall above Borobudur implies: there can be no doubt — Borobudur is a depiction of the three cosmic spheres reflecting the world of longing, matter and the non-material world, and it expresses the permutations of the soul as it frees itself of all dependence on matter and shape to reach the absolute, symbolized in the central Stupa.

'Accustomed to considering life now and in future as one and one alone, I lost my fear of birth and death'

Milarepa, born in 1052 (?), Tibetian poet and saint

It is not only the imposing size of these sculptures — the Buddha measures 3 metres (10 feet), Lokeśvara 2.4 metres (7 ft 10 in) and Vairapani 2.6 metres (8ft 6 in) — that overwhelms and attracts the visitor. It is far more a question of the special atmosphere of the entire interior, which seems to spring from the very spirit of the place. Even light and colour here speak a different, unknown but intimate-sounding tongue, and man, small as he is, feels good below these large statues and glad to light his humble lamp. Before he leaves, he raises his eyes to the ceiling — to the centre of the universe, in which the Buddha Śakyamuni rises as an eternal pattern.

147   Detail of the Buddha Śakyamuni.

148   A small lamp lit in honour of the Buddha, today as a thousand years ago.

149   The Bodhisattva Vairapani. ▶

150   View of the vaulted ceiling inside the pyramid-shaped temple with the statue of the Buddha. ▶ ▶

The siting of Borobudur, Chandi Pawon and Chandi Mendut

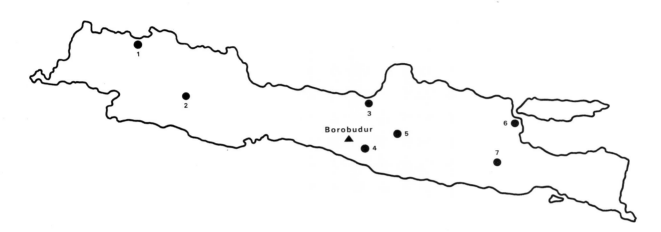

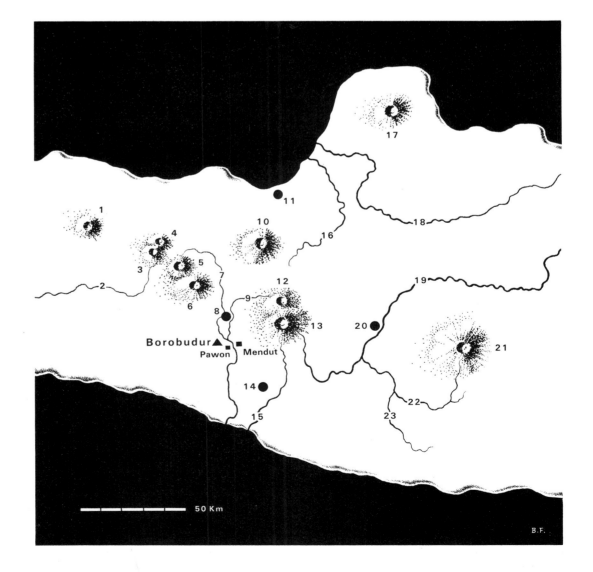

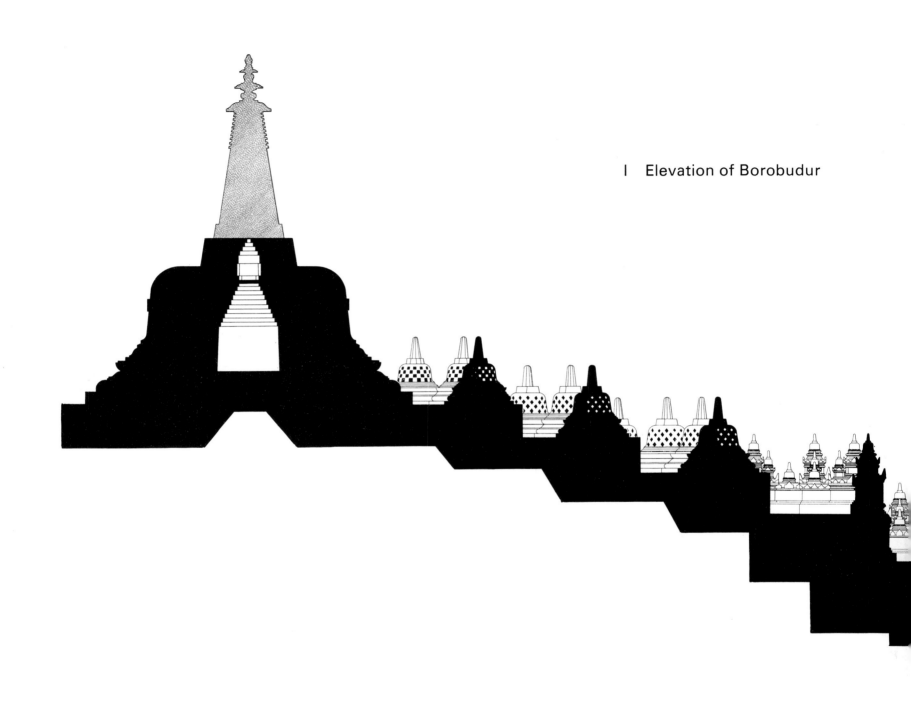

I   Elevation of Borobudur

lo m

Central stupa   3rd terrace   2nd terrace   1st terrace   Plateau   4th gall

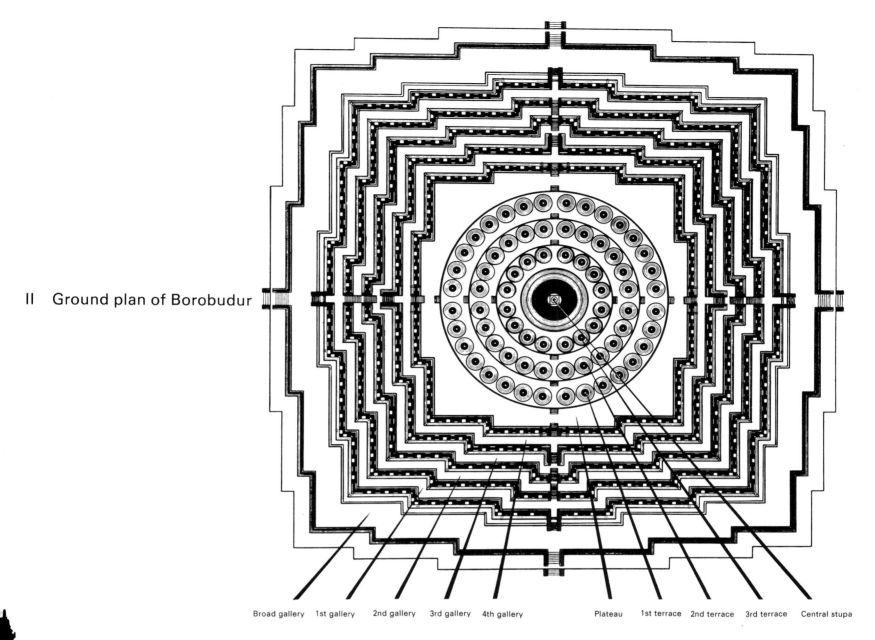

II   Ground plan of Borobudur

Broad gallery   1st gallery   2nd gallery   3rd gallery   4th gallery   Plateau   1st terrace   2nd terrace   3rd terrace   Central stupa

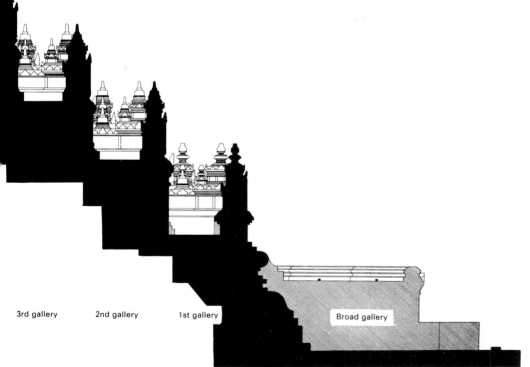

3rd gallery   2nd gallery   1st gallery   Broad gallery

131

Borobudur — a message in stone

Nowadays we expect every modern book dealing with ancient monuments to make some mention of the stars in the sky and ancient astronomy. The study of the orientation of objects of ancient times in relation to the cosmos has long assumed its place among the other, formerly preferred approaches.

Nobody will be surprised if we add Borobudur, that jewel of the southern hemisphere, to the other famous 'calendar buildings'. Borobudur is, however, a harder nut to crack than it might seem at first sight. This is a conclusion reached by many world-famous specialists. This sanctuary does not reveal its secret to anyone who comes along; and I am justified in saying and believing that its builders intentionally hid it so skilfully in order that it might not be found by the wrong hands or at the wrong time. One might even argue that the endless steps and stairways, and the kilometres of stone reliefs are arranged in such a manner as to confuse us in our calculations and to beguile us away from simple measuring and reasoning.

From the first tentative steps we take, we are overcome by a feeling that Borobudur might reveal to us far more than at first meets the eye. It seems to lead us on from step to step, and to relate its story and sing to us. And this is more than merely a poetical metaphor. The stone lace rises and sinks according to exactly the same laws that Ravi Shankar uses when he plays old Indian musical forms — the Ragas — on his sitar. After long calculations and analyses, I have reached the conclusion that it might be possible to write down in musical notes the entire architectonic complex that has otherwise been geodetically mapped in great detail.

In the octaves there appear the identical seven tones rising from the basic tone. They rise in bold ascents and return anew in soft descents to the one selected from the inner tones, which keep along the path to the desired goal those who are dubious or might fall by the wayside. In Borobudur, this danger arises by stops in front of the statues of the Buddha, all of which seem to be alike. They differ, however, in the symbolism of their gestures and their different ornaments.

The octaves of the Ragas can be spread over 22 soft minor tones. The figures 22 and 7 both play an important role in geometry to this day and literally pervade the entire structure, its sum-total and its smallest details. A role is played by right-angled triangles with sides expressed in small whole numbers that we hear about in the 'Salvasutras' ('Rules on the string and the bamboo pole') — in fact, a textbook of geometry used in laying out altars and sacred groves. We can find here practically all that the mathematician Mahavira wrote about in the ninth century AD: 'Reckoning is useful in every activity connected with secular, Vedic or other religious matters. The knowledge of counting is valued highly in matters of love, in an understanding of wealth, in music, drama, the art of cookery, in medicine, architecture and prosody, in verse composition and poetry, in logics and grammar and other things . . . It is used in connection with the movement of the Sun and other heavenly bodies, in the eclipse and conjunction of the planets and in connection with the search for the direction, position, time and movement of the Moon.'

This view is not to be wondered at if we realize that Buddha himself, as tradition has it, learnt to write and count at the age of eight. This 'hermetic' knowledge was open only to the chosen. It is known as 'hermetic' because in Greece it fell into the realm of the god Hermes; in ancient Rome it was the privilege of the god Mercury and in other countries it was, similarly, the right of the deities with jurisdiction over education, writing, trading and travel. Buddha, at the same time, is the Indian name for the planet Mercury as observed, according to Claudius Ptolemy, by the Greek Timochar in the year 265 BC — by strange coincidence, at the very time when the legendary propagator of Buddhism, King Asoka, lived (273—236 BC).

And so we might pose a number of fundamental questions. Does Borobudur encompass within itself the revival of a much older cult? Was there a renaissance of something that the builders of the Egyptian pyramids had already known and encoded in the little figures of scribes, until recently considered mere companions of their masters in posthumous life? Today we know that they contain the modules of measurements of length, often also of weight and volume and sometimes compositional schemes, for example, the statue of Senmut, the builder at the court of Queen Hatshepsut, or the little statue of the Mesopotamian ruler Gudey. And why does the Buddha sit in exactly the same posture as the scribes of the builders of the Egyptian pyramids? And what about the common love of both these cultures for the lotus? And where did the builders of Borobudur get the almost 5,500-year-old rules of composition? From where did they get the information that Buddha's altars are to keep to the same shape or volume? And why does the mother of Buddha — the Enlightened One, who lent her name to the planet Mercury — bear the name of Maya, which is identical with Maia, the mother of Hermes or Mercury?

Nor is it by chance that Borobudur stands at seven and a half degrees to the southern latitude. In this position, it is a grandiose gnomon, which the sun encircles on its yearly pilgrimage and lights up from all sides. It must have been a remarkable night observatory too, and perhaps helped to determine Ptolemy's 'platonic' year, which he put at 36,000 years, more precisely at 24,000 years, the measurement often used in Indian astrology until recently to define the 'Ajanamsi' (today given roughly as 26,000 years).

Almost directly overhead moves one of the brightest stars of the sky, Rigel, lying in the constellation of Orion, which so often, from Gilgamesh to the Odyssey, represents a hunter and who, in this role, presented Buddha with the garment of bast when he decided to lay aside his valuable robes adorned with jewelled stars of the Milky Way.

From Borobudur one can deduce astronomically the birth of the reyal Buddha's son Rahula, the star Regulus, that denotes the heart of the constellation of the Lion. The symbols of the lion on the Asoka columns spring to mind at once.

And if we remain at Borobudur until night falls, we can see that the Big and Little Bears turn into Elephants — the Great White Elephant lifts its trunk towards the sleeping Virgin to enchant her anew with the most beautiful of dreams.

Borobudur is an unread library of more than a thousand and one nights. And it is silently awaiting its listeners and readers.

Vratislav Jan Žižka

III Stupa, a devotional offering in memory of a pilgrimage or a votive offering. It was sometimes part of the foundation of a sacred building (see pictures 4 and 5). On the left, a view of the interior of the bronze bell resembling the ceiling in the cell of Mendut (see picture 150). In the centre, the general view of the pyramid that recalls Borobudur. On the top of the pyramid, there are eight Stupas of the Tibetan type centred around a central one — a total of nine Stupas, the sacred number of Buddhism. On the right, the view from the top (see the ground plan of Borobudur). This devotional offering does not come from Indonesia but from Tibet, the area of 'northern Buddhism', and is proof of the one-time similarities between Mahayana and northern Buddhism, arising from their common image of the cosmos. Baked clay, 85 × 85 mm, height 75 mm, private collection, Prague.

IV Similar devotionalia of Indonesian type. It used to be made in two parts: the upper part and the Stupa itself — here indicated by shading — on which Buddha or some other figure of the Buddhist pantheon was depicted in relief turned towards the interior of the Stupa. Here again we can find the symbolism known from the perforated Stupas of Borobudur: Buddha inside the Stupa, that is in the centre of the universe. The lower parts of two such devotionalia are shown in illustration 5.

V 'The Lotus — the Jewel on the Lake', reconstruction of the visual impression Borobudur would have made when surrounded by the lake. The authors used a drawing made by F.C. Wilson in 1850, which shows the temple in an idealized panorama but without a surrounding lake. (See page 12.)

Bibliography

Anand, Mulk Raj: *The Hindu View of Art.* Asia Publishing House, Bombay, 1957.

Auboyer, J. and Goepper, R.: *Landmarks of the World's Art: The Oriental World.* Paul Hamlyn Ltd., London, 1967.

Balsham, A. L.: *The Wonder that was India, A Survey of the Culture of the Indian Sub-Continent Before the Coming of the Muslims.* Grove Press, New York, 1959.

Barnett, L.: *Universe and Dr. Einstein,* Gollancz, London, 1949.

Bernet Kempers, A. J.: *The Bronzes of Nalanda and Hindu Javanese Art.* Bijdragen tot de Taal-, Land- en Volkenkunde (van Nederlandsch-Indie), XC-1933.

Bernet Kempers, A. J.: *Oud-Javaansche metaalkunst in de verzameling van Mr. J. G. Huyser.* Jaarboek N. I. O. N. 1935, 's-Gravenhage.

Bernet Kempers, A. J.: *Ancient Indonesian Art.* Harvard University Press, Cambridge, Massachusetts, 1959.

Bernet Kempers, A. J.: *Ageless Borobudur.* Servire/Wassenaar, 1976.

Born, M.: *The Restless Universe.* Dover Publication Co., New York, 1951.

Bosch, F. D. K.: *The Golden Germ* — An Introduction to Indian Symbolism. 's-Gravenhage, Mouton and Co., Den Haag, 1960.

Casparis, J. G. de: *New Evidence on Cultural Relations between Java and Ceylon in Ancient Times* (Artibus Asiae, XXIV, 1961).

Casparis, J. G. de: *Prasasti Indonesia,* Vol. I. A. C. Nix, Bandung, 1950.

Casparis, J. G. de: *Prasasti Indonesia,* Vol. II. Masa Buru, Bandung, 1956.

Christie, A. H.: *Splendours of the East.* (Chapters: South-East Asia, Cambodia — Angkor Wat, Burma — The Shwee Dagon, Indonesia — Borobudur), Weidenfeld and Nicolson, London, 1965.

Coedès, G.: *Les Etats Hindouisés d'Indochine et d'Indonésie.* E. de Boccard, Paris, 1964.

Covarrubias, M.: *Island of Bali.* Cassell and Co., Ltd., London, 1937.

Dekker Douwes, N. A.: *Tanah Air Kita.* N. V. Uitgeverij W. van Hoeve, 's-Gravenhage, Bandung.

Doehring, K.: *Indische Kunst* — *Einführung und Übersicht.* Deutsche Buchgemeinschaft, Berlin, 1926.

Fontein, J.: *Sepilgrimage of Suddhana.* 1966.

Fontein, J.: *Notes on the Jatacas and Avadanas of Barabudur:* An Arbor Papers (International Conference on Borobudur, An Arbor Michigan), 1974.

Geertz, C.: *The Religion of Java.* Glencoe, The Free Press, Illinois, 1960.

Glasenapp, H. von: *Buddhistische Misterien* — *Die geheimen Lehren und Ritten des Diamant-Fahrzeugs.* 1940.

Glasenapp, H. von: *Brahma und Buddha* — *Die Religionen Indiens in ihrer geschichtlichen Entwickelung.* Deutsche Buchgemeinschaft, Berlin, 1926.

Goloubew, V.: *L'Age du bronze au Tonkin et dans le Nord-Annam.* Bulletin de l'École Française d'Extrême-Orient 29/1929.

Heekeren, H. R. van: *The Bronze-Iron Age of Indonesia.* Nijhoff, The Hague, 1958.

Heeren-Palm C. H. M.: *Polynessche migraties.* 1955.

Heine-Geldern, R. von: *Altjavanische Bronzen aus dem Besitze der ethnographischen Sammlung des Naturhistorischen Museums in Wien.* C. W. Stern, Wien, 1925.

Heine-Geldern, R. von: *Vorgeschichtliche Grundlagen der Kolonialindischen Kunst,* Ibid. 8, 1933.

Heine-Geldern, R. von: 'Introduction' — Indonesian Art: a loan exhibition from the Royal Indies Institute, Amsterdam. Baltimore Museum of Art, Baltimore, 1949.

Hiss Hanson Ph.: *Bali.* R. Hale Ltd., London, 1941.

Indonesia Handbook. Department of Information, Republic of Indonesia, Jakarta, 1976.

Karlgren, B.: *The Date of early Dong-so'n Culture.* Bull. Mus. Far East. Antiq. No 14, Stockholm, 1942.

Krom, N. J.: *L'Art Javanais dans les Musées de Hollande et de Java.* G. van Oest, Paris/Brussel, 1923.

Krom, N. J.: *Lalitavistara.* De Levensgeschiedenis van den Buddha op Barabudur. M. Nijhoff, 's-Gravenhage, 1926.

Krom, N. J. en van Erp, T.: *Beschrijving van Barabudur,* I. Reliefs, II. Reliefs en Buddha-beelden. M. Nijhoff, 's-Gravenhage, 1920.

Krom, N. J. en van Erp T.: *Beschrijving van Barabudur,* Tweede deel, Bouwkundige Beschrijving door T. van Erp. M. Nijhoff, 's-Gravenhage, 1931.

Leemans, C.: *Boro-Boedoer op het Eiland Java,* afgebeeld en onder toezigt van F. C. Wilsen. 4 vols., E. J. Brill, Leiden, 1873.

Mookerjee, A. (With a Contribution by Philip Rawson): *Yoga Art.* Thames & Hudson, London, 1975.

Mookerjee, A.: *Tantra-Kunst, ihre Philosophie und Naturwissenschaft.* Ravi Kumar, Paris, Anton Schroll Verlag, Wien — München, 1967/68.

Munro, Th.: *Oriental Aesthetics.* Western Reserve University, Cleveland, 1965.

Munshi, K. M.: *Saga of Indian Sculpture.* Bharatiya Vidya Bhavan, Bombay, 1957.

Mus, P.: *Barabudur, Esquisse d'une histoire du Bouddhisme fondée sur la critique archéologique des textes.* Imprimerie d'Extrême Orient, Hanoi, 1935.

Ouspensky, P. D.: *New Model of the Universe.* Routlege, London, 1953.

Pott, P. H.: 'Le Bouddhisme de Java et l'Ancienne civilisation Javanaise', Serie Orientale Roma, V. (1952), Instituto Italiano per il Medio ed Estremo Oriente.

Raeburn, M.: *An outline of World Architecture.* Octopus Books, London, 1978.

Raffles, T. S.: *The History of Java.* 2 vols. Black, Parbury and Allen, London, 1817.

Rhodius, H.: Edition *Schönheit und Reichtum des Lebens,* Walter Spies, L. J. C. Boucher, Haag, 1964.

Rose, F. H.: *Meaning of Life in Hinduism and Buddhism.* Routledge & Kegan Paul, London, 1952.

Salmony, A.: *Der Borobudur in der Landschaft* ('Asien', Heft 12), Goltz Verlag München, 1921.

Scheltema, J. F.: *Monumental Java.* Macmillan and Co., Ltd., London, 1912.

Schrieke, B.: 'The End of Classical Hindu-Javanese Culture in Central Java', in his Indonesian Sociological Studies, Vol. II , Van Hoeve, The Hague, 1957.

Silva-Vigier, A. de: *The Life of the Buddha.* Retold from ancient sources. The Phaidon Press, London, 1955.

Speiser, W.: *Baukunst des Ostens.* Burkhard-Verlag Ernst Heyer, Essen, 1964.

Stutterheim, W. F.: *Rama Legenden und Rama Reliefs in Indonesien.* Bd. I. u. II., Georg Müller, München, 1925.

Stutterheim, W. F.: 'The Meaning of the Hindu-Javanese Candi', Journal of the American Oriental Society, LI, 1931.

Stutterheim, W. F.: *Het Hinduism in de Archipel.* Rev. ed. Cultuurgeschiedenis van Indonesie, II. Djakart, J. B. Wolters, Groningen, 1951.

Tagore, E.: *Religion of Man.* Allen & Unwin, London, 1949.

Tobi, A. C.: *De Buddhistische bronzen in het Museum te Leiden.* Oudheidkundig Verslag van de Oudheidkundige Dienst in Ned.-Indië, 1930.

Tucci, G.: *The Theory and Practice of the Mandala.* Rider & Co., London, 1961.

Vogel, J. Ph.: *The Relation between the Art of India and Java.* From 'The Influences of Indian Art', The India Society, London, 1925.

Vroklage, B. A. G.: *Das Schiff in den Megalithkulturen Südostasiens und der Südsee* ('Anthropos' XXXI —1936).

Wagner, F. A.: *Indonesien* (Kunst der Welt), Holle Verlag, Baden-Baden, 1959.

Wheeler, Mortimer: *Splendours of the East.* Weidenfeld and Nicolson, London, 1965.

With, K.: *Java* — *Brahmanische, Buddhistische und Eigenlebige Architektur und Plastik auf Java.* Folkwang Verlag, Hagen i. W., 1920.

Zimmer, H.: *The Art of Indian Asia, Its Mythology and Transformations.* Compiled and edited by Joseph Campbell, Pantheon Books, New York, 1955.

List of Illustrations

Photo No. 6 was loaned by Vladimír Sís. The photograph of the constellation Orion to the illustration 'Borobudur by night' (No. 135) was supplied by Petr Sojka. Some photos in the author's archive showing reliefs from which the moss and patina have been removed were made in the first quarter of the century by J. Cicvárek.